I0465646

DEDICATION

This book is dedicated to The Most High (TMH) for any ability I have. I am eternally grateful for the incredible family TMH has blessed me with. I might be biased, but I can't imagine having a better one. To be graced with a mom (thank you Mommy for sitting through every pie-in-the-sky idea with enthusiasm) and dad who makes me feel cherished is a profound blessing. My sisters (Monique and Kiki), whom I can genuinely call my best friends (thank you Mommy), are a constant source of support and joy. My adult children amaze me daily with their wisdom. To my sisters, and brothers from another mother (Stella Johnson, Somphien Amphone, Sister Mary Angela, Ernestine Curtis, Carolyn Ward, Tawnya Kitt, Rick Woods, and Sonja Bachus), your wisdom, bond, and love are invaluable treasures.

To my tried and true mentor, Arneatha Martin, who has passed from this earth but never from my heart, your guidance and wisdom continue to inspire me. To my teacher Momma Jill, thank you for your continued guidance, love, and support.

And I have saved the best for last: my husband, Clinton Lee. Your love and protection allow me to soar. As Uncle Paul said, I'm the one you would fight a bear for, and I have seen it and believe it. You are one of the greatest gifts that God has given me. Thank you for always giving me the room and freedom to grow.

To my clients, past and present, thank you for trusting me to guide you toward excellence. Your faith in me is a constant source of motivation.

Thank you all for your unwavering faith, encouragement, and guidance. You have been my anchor.

Title: Leading with Purpose: Executive Insights for Business Success and Personal Growth
Subtitle: Harnessing Decades of Leadership Experience
Author: Venus Lee

Copyright Notice: © 2025 Venus Lee. All rights reserved.
No part of this book may be reproduced or transmitted in any form or by any means, electronic or mechanical, including photocopying, recording, or by any information storage and retrieval system, without the written permission of the publisher, except where permitted by law.

Cover: © 2025 Venus Lee, generated by ChatGPT - OpenAI and modified by Crystal Johnson Turner.

Disclaimer: The information in this Book is provided for general informational purposes only. While the author has made every effort to ensure the accuracy of the information contained in this book, the author and publisher make no representations or warranties with respect to the accuracy or completeness of the contents of this book and specifically disclaim any implied warranties of merchantability or fitness for a particular purpose. The advice and strategies contained herein may not be suitable for every situation. You should consult with a professional where appropriate. The author shall not be liable for any loss of profit or any other commercial damages, including but not limited to special, incidental, consequential, or other damages.

Contact Information: Venus Lee & Associates, Inc.
Wichita, KS
Website: venusleeandassociates.com

TABLE OF CONTENTS

FOREWORD

Every now and then you meet someone who has an exceptional gift and talent that is able to transcend individual norms. A gift and talent filled with the wisdom and knowledge that enables companies and non-profits to revolutionize and revitalize their vision, mission, and purpose along with their doing. Venus Lee is that person.

From the first time I met her, I wanted to glean from her wisdom and knowledge. Ms. Lee gently informed me, "You see yourself as grasshoppers, but I see you as giants". From that point on I knew I wanted to begin to see my non-profit through her lens and I was so grateful that the opportunity had presented itself. Venus Lee questioned my methods, and challenged my thinking and my doing. She opened my eyes to the possibilities that existed before me, and I wanted what she envisioned because I could not see it as well. That is what her book will do for you.

In this Book, Venus shares her wealth of knowledge, offering readers a comprehensive guide to leadership that transcends traditional business strategies. Her unique approach, rooted in ethical integrity and visionary foresight, provides invaluable insights for leaders seeking to make a lasting positive impact.

As you journey through these pages, you will find not only practical advice but also profound life lessons that reflect Venus's personal experiences and professional triumphs. Whether you are an aspiring leader or a seasoned executive, this book will equip you with the tools to lead with purpose, inspire your team, and drive your organization towards enduring success.

Enjoy this enlightening journey.

By Min. Nina Shaw-Woody, LMSW
Executive Director
The Ministry of KFAN

SOFT INTRODUCTION - THE POWER OF CHANGE

I have always, from as far back as I can remember, seen the world through a story's lens. I visualize scenarios playing out in my head, seeing the intricate dynamics and potential outcomes. To start this journey, I want to share a fictional story with you. This narrative will help put you in the frame of mind to think strategically as you delve into the practical parts of this book.

The Power of Change

In the high-stakes world of corporate leadership, few stories are as compelling as that of CEO Jonathan Blake. Jonathan was a strikingly handsome black man, with a presence that turned heads and a charisma that could light up a room. His deep, soulful eyes and a smile that could win over the toughest critics had often been his secret weapon. Jonathan had built a reputation for transforming struggling businesses into thriving enterprises, seemingly with ease. However, his latest venture, a tech startup called InnovateX, was proving to be his greatest challenge yet.

Despite Jonathan's best efforts, InnovateX was plagued by internal conflicts and a stagnant growth trajectory. The board was growing restless, and Jonathan knew he needed help. Enter Vlylee Thomlee, a renowned consultant with a knack for turning around even the most troubled organizations. Vlylee's reputation preceded her—she was known for her unorthodox methods and her ability to inspire change from within.

Jonathan, with his characteristic charm, reached out to Vlylee with a sense of urgency. He needed someone who could not only diagnose the issues within his team but also implement sustainable solutions. Vlylee accepted the challenge, intrigued by the potential of InnovateX and the charisma of its CEO.

On her first day at InnovateX, Vlylee made an unassuming entrance. Dressed in a sleek, professional ensemble that hinted at her confident yet approachable demeanor, she was ready to dive in. Jonathan, with his natural charm, greeted her warmly, expecting to use his usual tactics to get her on his side. However, Vlylee saw right through him. She appreciated his attractiveness and charm but knew that it was his leadership skills that needed refining.

Vlylee's first move was to observe the team dynamics without disrupting the flow. She attended meetings, engaged in casual conversations, and took meticulous notes. It didn't take long for Vlylee to identify the core issues. The team was fragmented, with leaders operating in silos and a pervasive lack of trust. The company's vision was blurred by internal politics and misaligned priorities. Vlylee knew that to fix the team, she needed to get to the heart of these problems.

She scheduled one-on-one meetings with each team member, starting with Jonathan. In their conversation, Vlylee gently probed into his leadership style, his vision for InnovateX, and his frustrations. Jonathan, initially guarded, soon found himself opening up about his challenges and his hopes for the company.

"Jonathan," Vlylee said, leaning in with a reassuring smile, "change begins with you. Your team looks to you for direction, and if you're feeling lost, they will too. We need to realign your vision with your leadership."

Jonathan, used to his good looks and charm carrying him through tough situations, realized that Vlylee was different. She wasn't swayed by his external attributes; she saw the potential leader within him and was determined to bring that to the forefront.

Vlylee's approach was both direct and empathetic. She understood that leadership was as much about emotional intelligence as it was about strategic thinking. She worked with Jonathan to redefine his leadership style, emphasizing transparency, empathy, and accountability.

Next, Vlylee turned her attention to the broader team. She organized a series of workshops designed to rebuild trust and foster collaboration. These sessions were anything but typical corporate training. Vlylee incorporated elements of storytelling, encouraging team members to share their experiences and perspectives. This storytelling approach created a safe space for honest dialogue and mutual understanding.

In one particularly memorable session, Vlylee asked each leader to write down their vision for InnovateX on a piece of paper. They then shared these visions with the group, sparking a powerful conversation about alignment and purpose. Through these exercises, the team began to see each other not as competitors, but as collaborators working towards a common goal.

Vlylee also implemented regular feedback loops, where team members could voice their concerns and celebrate their successes. These sessions fostered a culture of continuous improvement and mutual support.

As the weeks passed, the transformation at InnovateX was palpable. The team was more cohesive, and their productivity soared. Jonathan, once overwhelmed by the weight of his role, now led with renewed confidence and clarity. The board, initially skeptical, began to see the positive changes reflected in the company's performance.

Vlylee's work at InnovateX was far from complete, but the foundation had been laid. The company's journey was a testament to the power of strategic intervention and the importance of a faith-driven, empathetic approach to leadership.

Leading with Purpose: Executive Insights for Business Success and Personal Growth

INTRODUCTION

Leadership is more than a title or a checklist of responsibilities — it's a journey of character, faith, and growth. Over the years, I've come to understand that true leadership isn't about knowing all the answers; it's about being willing to ask the right questions, to listen, and to keep learning.

In today's fast-paced business world, it's easy to get caught up in strategy, success metrics, and performance goals. But the essence of leadership extends beyond management or profit margins. It's about integrity when no one is watching, compassion when decisions get hard, and the courage to lead with both conviction and humility.

"Leading with Purpose" is not written from the seat of perfection but from the trenches of experience. After more than three decades in leadership and service — filled with triumphs, missteps, lessons, and second chances — I wanted to share what I've learned about leading with both excellence and grace. This book intertwines executive insight with spiritual truth because I've seen firsthand that faith has a way of steadying us when everything else shakes.

You won't find formulas here. Instead, you'll find reflections and real stories drawn from the boardroom and the prayer room alike — where vision meets vulnerability, and purpose meets perseverance. My hope is that as you turn these pages, you'll not only learn practical strategies for leadership but also feel permission to pause, to reflect, and to let your purpose lead you forward — one decision, one conversation, and one act of courage at a time.

CHAPTER 1: FOUNDATIONS OF FAITH-DRIVEN LEADERSHIP

Introduction

Leadership, at its best, is more than strategy, vision statements, or well-crafted goals. It's an act of faith — believing that the work you do can make a difference, even when the outcome is uncertain. I've sat in boardrooms where numbers told one story and the spirit whispered another. I've learned that real leadership is not about titles or applause; it's about conviction, compassion, and the quiet courage to do what's right when no one is watching.

Faith-driven leadership doesn't mean you have all the answers. It means you trust that there is purpose even in the unknown. It's about leading with principles instead of pride, choosing people over profit (although without margin, there is no mission), and allowing humility to guide you when ego tries to take over.

For me, faith has never been confined to Sunday mornings — it's been the light that steadied me in crises (even the self-made ones), the voice that reminded me to forgive when it would've been easier to walk away, and the strength that carried me through seasons when leadership felt more like survival than success.

In this chapter, I want to explore what it really means to lead with faith — not as a slogan, but as a living, breathing foundation for decision-making, resilience, and compassion.

Why Faith Matters in Leadership

A Moral Compass When It Matters Most

Faith provides a moral compass, but the test of leadership comes when that compass is challenged. Early in my career, I thought leadership meant having the right strategy. Later, I learned it means having the right heart.

There came a time — during one of the hardest seasons of my professional life — when faith had to move from theory to action. It was during the height of the pandemic, when uncertainty became our daily companion. Our community clinic served thousands of patients who relied on us for basic care, and suddenly the world shut down. Funding slowed. Fear grew. The easy choice would have been to cut services, furlough staff, or retreat into self-preservation. But the Spirit within me said, *stand firm.*

We decided we would not lay off a single person. We would not close our doors. Instead, we reimagined how to serve. We turned parking lots into testing zones, restructured teams overnight, and worked long days masked and prayerful. Executives put on gloves and assisted with vaccinations.

I still remember standing in the break room, surrounded by exhausted faces, and saying, "We may be stretched, but we are not broken. We were called for such a time as this."

Faith gave us the courage to hold the line when logic said it was impossible. And in the end, we not only survived — we grew stronger. When the crisis subsided, the community remembered that we *showed up*. That's the legacy of faith in leadership: it builds trust that outlives the storm.

Faith as a Source of Resilience

Resilience doesn't come from strength alone; it comes from surrender — from believing that your effort, when paired with purpose, can outlast the pressure.

Years before the pandemic, I faced another defining moment when our community discovered dangerous levels of contamination in the local water supply. The chemicals were invisible but deadly. Families were scared, and the fear was justified. As a leader, I didn't have the luxury of waiting for someone else to act. We had to respond — not because it was in our budget, but because it was in our *calling*.

We mobilized partnerships, rallied volunteers, and found donors willing to help fund blood screenings and testing for affected residents. I remember the heaviness in those documented community meetings — people, precious people, screaming at each other, at us out of fear. The responsibility was immense. But in that moment, I realized that leadership guided by faith is about *presence* — showing up even when the situation feels too heavy to carry. At one point for me, it wasn't about who was to blame, it was about what can I do, if anything at all.

The outcome wasn't perfect. There were days when I cried in my car before walking into work, as I had during the pandemic. But every time I wanted to quit, I felt that quiet reminder: *This is bigger than you. Keep going.*

Faith didn't remove the obstacles — it steadied me through them.

It became my anchor when the winds of criticism and fatigue tried to blow me off course.

Community-Centered Leadership

Faith-driven leadership always circles back to people — to the belief that business, healthcare, and community work are not separate lanes but threads of the same fabric.

When you lead with faith, your decisions start to ask a different question: not "What will this cost?" but "Who will this serve?"

During my years leading a large community clinic, we often faced competing demands — grow faster, expand services, meet metrics. But I found that the most transformative initiatives were the ones rooted in compassion. We launched outreach programs that connected medical, dental, pharmacy, optometry, medical-legal and behavioral health care under one roof, because faith told us that healing isn't one-dimensional.

Later, during the pandemic, that same spirit pushed us beyond the walls of the clinic. We organized drive-up vaccination events and Pastor Don provided in house food distributions for our staff. We bumped up our services to the unhoused. We were never afraid to pray with people who were too afraid and undecided on the best course of treatment.

Faith reminded us that leadership isn't about authority — it's about accountability. And our community saw that we were not just providing healthcare; we were providing hope.

Integrating Faith and Professional Ethics
Values That Outlast Pressure

Integrating faith into leadership isn't about imposing belief; it's

about aligning values. Every organization I've worked with —
whether corporate or nonprofit — eventually faces the moment
when it must choose between what's right and what's easy.

In those moments, faith becomes the quiet voice that says,
Remember why you started.

I've walked executives through redefining mission statements
that used to sound polished but hollow. One team replaced
"growth and innovation" with "healing and stewardship."
Another replaced "industry excellence" with "integrity and
community impact." These weren't just words on paper; they
changed how decisions were made, how people were treated, and
how accountability was measured.

When faith informs ethics, the result isn't rigidity — it's clarity.
It helps teams lead with conscience instead of just compliance,
creating environments where people trust leadership because
they can *see* the alignment between words and actions.

The Compassion Factor

There's a common misconception that faith and empathy make
leaders soft. The truth is, they make leaders *stronger.* Compassion
(real compassion, not the fake compassion, that has no
accountability) doesn't weaken authority; it deepens influence.

I once worked with a group of administrators who were drained —
not because they lacked skill, but because they'd given every ounce
of themselves to caring for others. The weight of burnout was
palpable. Instead of diving into metrics or policies, we sat together
in a circle, no titles, no hierarchy — just people. I asked everyone to
share why they chose this work in the first place.

The tears flowed, and so did the healing. For some, it was the first time they'd been seen in months. From that day forward, something shifted. Morale improved. Client care improved. Not because of a new strategy, but because compassion had reentered the room.

That's what faith-driven leadership looks like: seeing beyond the surface, leading with both conviction and tenderness. It's what Yahusha modeled — truth and grace in equal measure.

Conclusion

Faith-driven leadership is not a trend or a tactic — it's a way of being. It calls us to lead with humility, to serve with integrity, and to love without condition.

Faith gives you a compass when the path disappears, strength when you feel unqualified, and grace when you've been misunderstood. It's what allows leaders to rise after failure, to rebuild after loss, and to continue believing in people when others have given up.

As I look back on the hardest seasons of my leadership journey — pandemics, crises, betrayals, breakthroughs — I see one constant thread: faith made me resilient, not invincible; compassionate, not naïve; steadfast, not stubborn.

If leadership is the bridge between vision and reality, then faith is the foundation that keeps it standing.

Let this be your reminder: You don't have to have all the answers to lead with purpose. You only have to be willing to trust, to listen, and to keep showing up — faithfully.

CHAPTER 2:
STRATEGIC PLANNING
AND EXECUTION

Introduction

Strategic planning is often misunderstood. Some leaders treat it as a binder full of charts and deadlines — a neatly organized prediction of the future. But the truth is, strategy isn't just about what's written down; it's about what's *lived out.*

Over the years, I've learned that a strategic plan is only as strong as the integrity and faith of those who carry it forward. In business, healthcare, or community work, strategy without values is fragile. Faith-driven strategy, on the other hand, creates direction that can withstand uncertainty, change, and even failure.

At my consultancy, I often tell clients that planning and execution must be more than procedural — they must be *purposeful.* Purpose gives strategy breath. Without it, teams chase outcomes but lose their "why."

When I sit with executive teams, whether in healthcare, nonprofit, or corporate settings, I don't just ask them about their goals; I ask, *"Who are you becoming as you reach for them?"* Because the future of an organization doesn't just depend on what it achieves — it depends on the character it preserves in the process.

This chapter is about aligning the head and the heart of leadership — pairing faith-inspired conviction with practical, measurable strategy. It's a reminder that a plan rooted in faith doesn't ignore reality; it interprets it through hope and responsibility.

The Importance of Ethical Strategic Planning

Building Strategy on Values, Not Just Vision

Every organization wants to grow, but not all growth is good growth.

Ethical strategic planning asks the harder questions:

- *Will this expansion align with our mission?*
- *Will it strengthen our community or just our metrics?*
- *Who benefits, and who might be left behind?*

When I guide clients through the planning process, we begin not with budgets or timelines, but with **values.** Before there's a single chart on the wall, I ask them to name the principles they refuse to compromise. From there, we design the plan *around* those non-negotiables.

For example, I once worked with a small clinic preparing to expand its services into underserved neighborhoods. They were excited — and understandably so. But they were also nervous about overextending financially. Instead of rushing to draft a five-year plan, I asked the team to pause. "Let's revisit your mission," I said. "What's driving this expansion — compassion or competition?"

That moment of pause changed everything. We reframed the plan through three guiding truths: serve the vulnerable first, remain debt-conscious, and protect staff well-being. Once those anchors were clear, the logistics naturally aligned. The expansion succeeded — not because of the perfect spreadsheet, but because faith and ethics guided every decision.

Faith-based strategy demands patience and introspection before projection. It's the discipline of saying, "We can — but should we?"

Turning Obstacles into Opportunities

One of the hardest parts of strategic planning is leading through tension — when the vision feels bigger than the resources, or when unexpected barriers threaten the plan.

In those moments, I remind leaders that strategy is not about control; it's about stewardship. Faith teaches us to lead with both confidence and surrender — doing our part while trusting Yah to open doors we cannot.

I once guided a nonprofit that was struggling to sustain its programs after a major grant ended. The executive director was anxious, and the board was divided about what to cut. Instead of starting with what they *couldn't* afford, I asked them to name what they *couldn't afford to lose.*

That conversation changed the trajectory of their planning. Together, we identified the programs that had the deepest community impact — the ones aligned with their calling. We then created an adaptive funding plan, diversifying revenue streams through local partnerships and new community collaborations.

It worked. But more importantly, it restored unity and peace within their team. They remembered why they started.

Sometimes, the best strategic plan doesn't begin with abundance; it begins with conviction.

Faith as a Filter for Decision-Making

When faith is integrated into planning, it becomes the filter that clarifies every decision.

In my own leadership journey, I learned to ask three questions before approving any initiative:

1. **Does this honor the mission?**
2. **Does this strengthen people — not just processes (although important)?**
3. **Would I still make this decision if no one ever praised it (hmmm...)?**

Those questions may seem simple, but I believe they save organizations from unwise expansions, poor partnerships, and short-sighted investments.

In one instance, I advised a leadership team that was considering a partnership promising fast revenue but questionable ethics. The data looked great — projections were up, and the board was eager. But as we prayed and reviewed the fine print, something didn't sit right.

Eventually, we discovered that the agreement would have compromised client confidentiality. Declining the offer cost them a short-term boost, but it preserved their reputation and integrity.

A faithful strategy sees beyond the next quarter. It asks, *What will this decision mean for us five years from now? For the people who trust us? For the story we'll tell when this chapter closes?*

Executing Strategic Plans with Integrity
The Human Side of Implementation

A plan looks clean on paper, but execution is messy. Real

leadership is what happens when the ink dries and the reality begins.

I often tell clients that executing a plan with integrity starts with **communication (with who and timing is everything) and inclusion (with who and timing is everything).** The most strategic thing a leader can do is make sure their people understand not just *what* they're doing, but *why.*

When consulting with organizations through transitions or expansions, I encourage leaders to slow down enough to bring their teams along emotionally and mentally. Faith-driven execution honors people as partners (this only works if you have the right people on the bus – a story for another day), not pawns.

I once helped a community agency restructure its departments. The changes were necessary but painful. Instead of rolling out the new model overnight, we scheduled open forums, created anonymous Q&A channels, and held weekly prayer or reflection sessions for staff who wanted spiritual grounding through the change.

Those moments of transparency didn't eliminate tension, but they cultivated trust. People can endure almost anything when they believe their leaders are honest and care about them.

Integrity in execution means walking your talk — even when progress is slower because you're doing it the right way.

Adaptability: Planning for What You Can't Predict

No strategic plan survives unchanged. I've seen the most beautiful plans unravel under the weight of unexpected events — pandemics, leadership transitions, market shifts, or community crises. But when faith is built into the plan, adaptation becomes a strength, not a setback.

At my consultancy, I teach teams to build **living plans.** These are strategies with breathing room — designed for learning, feedback, and adjustment.

For example, one organization I guided created a five-year plan but revisited it quarterly with a faith-based reflection session. We didn't just ask, "How are we performing?" We asked, "How are we *aligning*?" This rhythm turned the plan into a dialogue — a relationship between mission and progress.

When a supply issue disrupted their operations, they didn't panic; they pivoted. Because their plan was flexible, they could shift priorities quickly while staying anchored in their values.

Faith-inspired planning allows leaders to bend without breaking. It reminds us that Yahusha is in the details we cannot see, and that flexibility rooted in faith leads to sustainability rooted in peace.

Execution Through Collaboration and Accountability

Strategy fails when accountability fades (if this was an audio book, I would shout this out at the top of my lungs!). But accountability is not punishment — it's stewardship (Yes!!! Read it out loud – stewardship!).

In every consulting engagement, I ask leadership teams two accountability questions:

1. *Who will own this?*
2. *Who will hold this accountable with grace?*

Faith-driven leaders don't avoid accountability; they invite it. They understand that correction is not condemnation — it's refinement.

One of the most rewarding seasons of my consultancy work involved mentoring a leadership team that was learning to hold each other accountable in love. They created what we called "truth tables" — monthly check-ins where anyone could raise concerns about strategy execution, financial stewardship, or cultural drift. The rule was simple: speak truth with kindness (keep in mind that the receiver depending on where they are in their leadership may not interrupt it as kindness – you can't control that), listen without defensiveness (breathe), and pray before responding (this could save your career).

Over time, those meetings became a model for other departments. Conflicts decreased. Transparency increased.

And the organization began to flourish, not because of more funding, but because they trusted each other enough to tell the truth.

Integrity in execution is faith in motion — the courage to keep promises and the humility to admit when you've fallen short (I can almost feel the closing of books everywhere).

Conclusion

Strategic planning and execution are not just organizational disciplines; they're spiritual disciplines. They call us to be visionaries who plan with intention, act with conviction, and adapt with grace.

When you plan with faith, you stop chasing perfection and start pursuing alignment. You understand that success is not just about the finish line, but about how you walk the path — with integrity, compassion, and courage.

As a consultant, I often close planning sessions by asking leaders to pause and reflect – for teams that I feel are open to this – not everyone is open to this process – use wisdom:

When your next decision tests your values, what will guide you? When growth feels risky, will you trust your purpose more than your fear? When your plan requires faith to sustain it, will you still say yes?

Faith-based strategy invites you to lead from both head and heart — to see spreadsheets and souls at the same time.

And as you plan the next chapter of your leadership journey, remember: the best strategy doesn't start with "how much" — it starts with *why.*

So I'll leave you with this:
What would you do — if you planned not just for success, but for significance?

CHAPTER 3: EMPATHY AND EXECUTIVE COACHING

Introduction

Empathy. It sounds simple until you try to lead with it. Everyone loves the *idea* of being an empathetic leader — until empathy asks for patience when you're tired, grace when you're frustrated, and listening when you'd rather talk.

I've learned over time that empathy isn't weakness; it's wisdom. It's the quiet strength to understand without always agreeing, to connect without losing your boundaries, and to hold space for people even when they're hard to hold (so very hard to hold).

When I began coaching leaders, I used to think empathy was something we added *after* the strategy was built — a nice touch, a "soft skill." But years of sitting with executives, clinicians, and administrators have taught me that empathy is not the soft part of leadership — it's the structural beam that holds the weight of everything else.

This chapter will walk through what empathy really looks like in executive coaching and leadership development. We'll explore how it shapes decision-making, why it's often misunderstood, and how faith keeps it anchored. Because if strategy builds direction, empathy builds connection — and leadership without connection eventually collapses under its own brilliance.

Understanding Empathy in Leadership

Seeing Beyond the Surface

True empathy requires more than hearing; it requires seeing. When I sit across from a client — a CEO who feels overwhelmed, a manager frustrated with their team, or a new executive afraid they're in over their head — I remind myself: "This person isn't their title, and this moment isn't their whole story."

Faith teaches us that Yahusha looked *through* people, not just *at* them. He saw the potential buried under fear, pride, or failure — and called it forward. That's what empathetic leadership does: it calls out the good in others even when they can't see it themselves.

I once coached a senior leader who had a reputation for being "tough." When her staff described her, they used words like *intense*, *demanding*, and *unapproachable.* She didn't disagree — she laughed and said, "Venus, they're not wrong." (I appreciated her honesty!)

Instead of lecturing her, I asked her to tell me about the moment she first learned to protect herself. She paused, looked down, and said quietly, "When I realized no one was protecting me."
That was the turning point. Once we got to *that* truth, empathy started to flow both ways.

Empathy in leadership starts with curiosity — the willingness to ask, "What happened here?" instead of "What's wrong with you (I made that mistake once, okay, maybe twice)?"

The Cost of Leading Without Empathy

When empathy goes missing, leaders begin to lead by metrics instead of meaning. Productivity may go up for a while, but morale and creativity quietly die.

I've seen organizations where employees show up on time, hit every target, and go home empty. No joy, no loyalty, no spark. It's not burnout; it's *numbness.*

In one coaching engagement, a leader told me, "My people don't care anymore." I smiled gently and replied, "They probably do — they just don't think it matters anymore."

We walked through how empathy could be rebuilt, one honest conversation at a time.
He started holding five-minute check-ins (no check-ins = no buy-ins, and no trust) — not to measure output but to ask, "How are you holding up?" At first, the silence was awkward. (If this had been an audiobook, I'd insert that cringy pause sound effect right here.) But after a few weeks, his team began to talk — about burnout, about home life, about hope. Productivity came back naturally because people felt *seen.*

Empathy doesn't lower standards — it raises commitment.

Integrating Empathy into Executive Coaching
Coaching as Mirror and Ministry
Executive coaching isn't therapy, but it's definitely soul work. The goal isn't to fix people; it's to help them see themselves clearly and choose growth intentionally.

When clients come to me for coaching, I remind them that this isn't about performance polishing — it's about alignment. We look at how they treat people when they're under pressure, how they handle feedback, how they recover from mistakes. Those moments reveal character more than any résumé ever could.

Sometimes, I'll ask, "If your team could describe your leadership in one word, what would it be?" (Pause. Deep breath. You can practically hear their heartbeat at that point.)
The answers are rarely what they expected — and that's where the work begins.

Empathy turns coaching into partnership. It allows me to encourage clients without breaking them, to hold them accountable while protecting their dignity (although in one case, instead of dignity, a client told me that he felt castrated – yikes! Pay attention to your delivery method).

And faith keeps me grounded through it. Because let's be honest — there are days when coaching can feel like talking to a wall made of spreadsheets and pride. (I say that with love!) But prayer before those sessions has softened more hearts than any leadership model I could ever draw on a whiteboard (oh...and how I love my whiteboards).

Techniques That Build Empathy

There are a few simple — not easy, but simple — ways to cultivate empathy through coaching:

1. **Active Listening:** Not listening to respond, but listening to *understand.* This means leaving space for silence and resisting the urge to "fix" everything immediately (can anyone say, guilty over here).

    ◦ Sometimes leaders need to hear their own words echo before they realize what's really going on (trust me when I say, when they replay that recorder back in their head, you want it to be their words and not yours).

2. **Role Reversal Exercises:** I'll often have leaders imagine being on the receiving end of their own email, meeting, or tone. The results? Eye-opening — and occasionally hilarious. ("Wow, I'd probably ignore me too," one client admitted.)

3. **The Empathy Audit:** Every quarter, I ask clients to evaluate how well they've supported the people they lead. Not performance reviews — *relationship reviews.* Who have you encouraged? Who have you overlooked? Who needs a second chance?

4. **Faith Moments:** For those open to it, I close sessions with a prayer or reflection, inviting Yah to reveal blind spots or soften hearts. Some of the most powerful breakthroughs I've seen didn't come from strategy but surrender.

Empathy can be taught, but it must also be *caught* — modeled, lived, and reinforced in daily interactions.

Lessons from the Field

Empathy in action rarely looks glamorous. It's often messy, inconvenient, and underappreciated — until the results speak for themselves.

A few years ago, I was coaching a mid-level manager who struggled to lead her team through change. She was sharp, organized, and overworked — and she couldn't understand why her people resisted her directives.

When we unpacked it together, I discovered she hadn't stopped long enough to acknowledge the anxiety her staff felt. They weren't rebelling; they were scared.

We practiced empathy-based communication: starting team meetings with gratitude, asking for input instead of delivering decrees, and taking time to celebrate small wins.

Six months later, the same staff who once resisted her now defended her in meetings. Why? Because she learned to see them, not just manage them.

Another time, I worked with a board that was fractured after a conflict between leadership and staff. We spent hours peeling back layers of misunderstanding. At one point, someone said, "We just need to talk like humans again." (Amen.) That meeting ended with laughter — and prayer.

Empathy isn't a miracle cure, but it's often the first step toward healing.

Conclusion

Empathy is not weakness — it's the strength to feel without folding, to care without losing clarity. It's what allows leaders to carry both vision and vulnerability.

When we integrate empathy into leadership, we restore the human heartbeat to the work we do. Strategy gives direction, but empathy gives meaning.

So, as you step into your own leadership or coaching role, ask yourself:

- Who needs you to listen longer before you lead louder?
- Who around you feels unseen but still shows up anyway?
- Where might Yah be inviting you to soften — not so you

lose authority, but so you gain connection?

Empathy and faith walk hand in hand. One teaches you to love people as they are; the other reminds you to believe in who they can become.

And if you remember nothing else from this chapter, remember this:
A leader without empathy may gain compliance, but a leader with empathy inspires transformation.

Now pause for a moment — yes, actually pause — and ask yourself:
How do I want people to feel after they've experienced my leadership?

That question, more than any performance review or quarterly report, will tell you everything about the kind of leader you're becoming (hmmm....Got it?!).

CHAPTER 4: OPERATIONAL EXCELLENCE IN PRACTICE

Introduction

Operational excellence is not about perfection; it's about presence. It's about the ability to stay steady in chaos, to lead systems with both logic and love, and to remind people that behind every process is a person.

When I first stepped into operational leadership, I thought excellence meant speed, precision, and results. But faith — and a few humbling experiences — taught me that excellence is more than efficiency. It's consistency with character.

You can automate a workflow, but you can't automate integrity. You can optimize systems, but you can't shortcut stewardship. Real operational excellence begins when leaders stop asking, "How fast can we get this done?" and start asking, "How well can we do this *with purpose*?"

This chapter explores what that journey looks like from the inside. I've lived through the long nights, the spreadsheets that refused to balance, and the hallway conversations that changed everything.

The lessons here weren't learned in a seminar; they were earned — through trial, prayer, and grace.

Principles of Operational Excellence

1. Excellence Starts with Clarity

People don't resist change; they resist confusion. One of the hardest things I had to learn as a leader was that my excitement about a new initiative didn't automatically translate into understanding for everyone else. (If this were an audiobook, you'd probably hear me sigh right here.)

I remember implementing a new electronic system that promised to "streamline everything." Well… it didn't. Not at first. It created chaos, frustration, and a few side-eyes in staff meetings. The problem wasn't the system — it was the rollout. I hadn't slowed down enough to bring the right people along at the right time – buy-in at every stage, to prevent sabotage (don't find out the hard way that people and timing is everything – really know your team – the good, the bad, and the ugly – not everyone who smiles for you, are for you).

Excellence requires clarity — clear purpose, clear process, and clear communication. I learned to say, "Here's *why* we're doing this, and here's *how* it connects to our mission." Once people could see the heart behind the change, the resistance turned into ownership.

Faith taught me that vision without communication is assumption — and assumption is the fastest way to lose people who actually want to believe in you (c.r.a.p.! Okay, get over it, and let's keep it moving).

2. Stewardship Over Speed

There's always pressure to do more, faster, cheaper. But I've learned that stewardship trumps speed every time.

Operational excellence is not about running ahead of your capacity; it's about being faithful with what you have. During one season, we faced a resource shortage that made expansion nearly impossible. Every instinct in me said, *push harder,* but my spirit said, *protect what's already been entrusted to you.*

So instead of chasing every new idea, we focused on refining the systems we already had — simplifying paperwork, re-training staff, tightening supply processes, and revisiting our data flow. Within six months, efficiency improved and staff satisfaction rose. We didn't grow wider; we grew deeper.

Stewardship is spiritual maturity in motion — doing less with excellence instead of more with exhaustion.

3. Culture Eats Process (Every Single Time)

By the way, 'Culture Eats Process' is a misquote of Peter Drucker (okay, just want to get that out of the way). You can have the best processes in the world, but if your team culture is toxic, those processes will collapse under the weight of distrust.

I learned this lesson the hard way. Early in my career, I led a department full of brilliant people who couldn't work together. Meetings were polite but tense. Communication was transactional. Everything looked fine on paper — but it *felt* heavy.

One day, I stopped the agenda mid-meeting and said, "We can't keep pretending this is okay. We have to talk about how we're showing up." That conversation changed the direction of our department. We began addressing unspoken frustrations, rebuilding trust, and praying together at the start of meetings.

Slowly, the tension broke. Productivity went up — not because the process changed, but because the people did.

Culture is what carries excellence when systems are stressed.

Driving Innovation in Operations

Faith-Fueled Innovation

Innovation doesn't always start with invention; sometimes it starts with frustration. Some of the best ideas are born from leaders who are tired of saying, "There has to be a better way."

Faith allows us to see problems as possibilities. When things aren't working, instead of panicking, I ask, "What is Yah trying to teach or reveal here?" That question has saved me from making reactive decisions more times than I can count.

I remember when we needed to serve more patients without adding more space or staff. The math didn't work — but faith and creativity did. We rearranged schedules, cross-trained employees, and used technology to triage non-urgent visits. We served more people with the same resources and better morale. That's the miracle of operational excellence — it multiplies what you already have through wisdom and willingness.

The Human Side of Systems

People forget that operations are emotional. Every new form, every policy change, every scheduling tweak affects someone's daily rhythm. Leaders who ignore that reality may win efficiency but lose empathy.

I learned to pair every process change with a compassion check: "How will this affect people's time, energy, and peace?" Sometimes the answer forced me to redesign the plan entirely.

There's a running joke among my former staff that if you came to me with a process improvement idea, I'd ask two questions:
1. "Does it make life better for the people we serve?"
2. "Does it make life better for the people doing the serving?"

If the answer to either was no — back to the drawing board.

Faith-driven operations put people before performance — and ironically, that's what creates sustainable performance.

Another Short Story: Vlylee Thomlee and Mr. Clue - The Journey to Operational Excellence

Vlylee Thomlee, the sharp-eyed consultant known for her ability to untangle the most convoluted business knots, was on her way to meet Mr. Clue, a CEO who had built his company from the ground up. The company, a mid-sized manufacturing firm known for its innovative products, had hit a roadblock. Operational inefficiencies were starting to rear their ugly head, and the company's growth had plateaued. Mr. Clue, a man who had always prided himself on having all the answers, was stumped.

Mr. Clue was a tall, striking figure with a presence that commanded attention. His chiseled features and piercing eyes had always given him an edge in boardrooms, where his natural charisma and good looks often won over even the toughest of critics. But this time, his charm wasn't enough to pull him through the crisis at hand. The company he had nurtured was now on shaky ground, and the smooth-talking CEO found himself at a loss.

As Vlylee walked into Mr. Clue's office, she could sense the tension in the air. Mr. Clue greeted her with a firm handshake, his demeanor polished but the worry lines on his face betraying his unease.

"Vlylee, thank you for coming. We've got a bit of a mess on our hands, and I'm hoping you can help us clean it up," Mr. Clue said, his voice betraying the slightest hint of desperation.

Vlylee smiled warmly, but there was a steely resolve behind her eyes. "I'm here to help, Mr. Clue. Let's start by getting to the root of the problem."

Mr. Clue led her through the plant, explaining the operational issues they were facing—bottlenecks in production, declining quality, and missed delivery deadlines. Vlylee listened intently, asking pointed questions that made Mr. Clue realize that she saw right through the superficial charm and into the heart of the issues.

They settled into a conference room, and Vlylee pulled out her notebook. "Mr. Clue, your company has grown rapidly, and with that growth, the complexities of your operations have increased as well. What we're seeing here is a classic case of operational inefficiency—a result of trying to scale without adapting your processes accordingly."

Mr. Clue nodded. He knew she was right. His usual approach of relying on instinct and charisma had reached its limits. "What do you suggest?" he asked, his tone more respectful than before.

Vlylee leaned forward, her voice steady and confident. "First, we need to address efficiency while maintaining ethical standards. This isn't just about speeding up production; it's about doing so without compromising on the quality that your brand is known for. We'll start by streamlining your production process, much like I did with a healthcare client at an urgent care center. They were facing similar issues—long wait times and patient dissatisfaction. By redesigning their intake process, we improved throughput while ensuring patient care remained top-notch."

Mr. Clue was intrigued. "How does that apply here?"

"Think of your production line as the patient intake process. We'll identify the bottlenecks, remove unnecessary steps, and ensure that each phase of production is optimized for both speed and quality. This might mean investing in new technology, much like how we introduced electronic health records at that clinic to streamline data management."

As Vlylee spoke, Mr. Clue could see the plan unfolding in his mind. He realized that her approach was not just about fixing the immediate issues but about creating a sustainable model for long-term success.

"We'll also need to foster a culture of continuous improvement," Vlylee continued. "In healthcare, this often involves training sessions for staff to enhance patient care practices. In your case, it could mean leadership workshops and employee engagement programs that encourage innovation and efficiency at every level of your organization."

Mr. Clue leaned back in his chair, feeling a weight lift off his shoulders. He could see that Vlylee's strategy was exactly what his company needed. But there was more to it than that—he realized that he had underestimated her. Her intelligence, her insight, and her ability to see through the facade of the situation made her a force to be reckoned with.

"Vlylee, you've given me a lot to think about. I have to admit, I thought this would be a quick fix, but I see now that it's going to require some real work and commitment," Mr. Clue said, a newfound respect in his voice.

Vlylee smiled. "Operational excellence isn't achieved overnight, Mr. Clue. It's a journey. But with the right strategies and a commitment to continuous improvement, I'm confident we can get your company back on track."

Mr. Clue nodded, a determined look in his eyes. "Let's do it. Let's make this company better than it's ever been."

As they shook hands, Vlylee knew that this was the beginning of a transformative journey—not just for Mr. Clue's company but for Mr. Clue himself. And as for Mr. Clue, he realized that sometimes it takes more than charm and good looks to succeed—it takes a willingness to see the truth, to learn, and to grow.

And with Vlylee Thomlee by his side, he was ready to do just that.

Reflections from the Story

Every time I reread that story, I smile — partly because it's a little too familiar. I've been both characters: the one trying to fix everything and the one pretending to have it all under control.

Mr. Clue represents every leader who wants to do right but forgets that charisma doesn't fix culture. Vlylee reminds me of the kind of leader I aspire to be — observant, patient, faith-anchored, and not afraid to say, "This might take longer, but it'll be worth it."

And if I may pause here for a real-world note: I've been told before — more than once — that I should "tone down" what I know, so others can feel comfortable shining. As a consultant, I've learned that is not humility; that's suppression. Our responsibility is to *serve with knowledge,* not shrink from it. When I don't know something, I say so, and I find out. But when I do know — especially through decades of hard-earned experience — it would dishonor both the work and the calling to pretend otherwise.

For women, and especially Black women, this request to minimize our mastery often comes dressed as advice. But excellence doesn't dim to make others comfortable — it teaches, it uplifts, it creates space for everyone to grow. That's what faithful leadership does: it doesn't overshadow; it illuminates.

Operational excellence isn't about looking like the smartest person in the room. It's about being the most faithful person in the room — the one who will stay long enough to finish what others start, refine what others overlook, and nurture what others neglect.

Conclusion

Operational excellence is faith expressed through consistency. It's not glamorous, but it's sacred work — the daily discipline of creating order out of chaos, compassion out of process, and peace out of pressure.

When systems run smoothly, people feel safe enough to do their best work. That's leadership. That's ministry.

So as you reflect on this chapter, ask yourself:

- What does excellence mean in your daily work — not the corporate definition, but *your* definition?
- Where can you simplify instead of stretch?

- And how can you bring more faith and less fear into the systems you lead?

Operational excellence begins with stewardship and ends with gratitude. It's knowing that every spreadsheet, every process, and every person is part of something much bigger than the task at hand.

And if no one else tells you this, hear it from me: **Excellence isn't about perfection — it's about presence. Show up, stay faithful, and the systems will follow.**

CHAPTER 5:
NAVIGATING
COMPLIANCE
AND RISK

Introduction

If there's one topic that can make even the most confident leader sigh, it's compliance. Just the word itself has a way of drying out the room. But here's the truth — compliance, when done right, is not about restriction. It's about protection. It's the fence that keeps the mission safe.

In leadership, especially in healthcare and community service, compliance isn't the glamorous part of the job — it's the backbone. It's what allows organizations to serve with integrity and sleep at night knowing their good intentions won't unravel into chaos tomorrow.

I used to think compliance was mostly about checking boxes and surviving audits. (Let's be honest, many of us have prayed our way through one or two of those!) But experience taught me something deeper: compliance is a leadership mindset. It's about *honoring the trust* people place in us — patients, employees, partners, and funders alike.

And risk? Risk is the reality that keeps us humble. You can have the best systems in the world and still find yourself blindsided by the one thing you didn't see coming. But faith has a way of steadying us in both. It teaches us to lead responsibly while trusting Yahusha with what's beyond our control.

So, let's dive into what it means to navigate compliance and risk — not as a chore, but as a calling.

Understanding Compliance and Risk Management
The Foundation of Integrity

Compliance begins with culture, not policy. If you build a culture that values honesty, accountability, and transparency, most compliance issues solve themselves long before a manual or matrix gets involved, although important.

I've seen leaders obsess over binders, training slides, and flowcharts (and I love a good flowchart!), but neglect the everyday conversations that shape behavior. A well-trained team can still go astray if the culture rewards silence over truth.

One of the first things I teach in consulting is this: **"Documents don't keep you compliant — people do."** It's not enough for staff to know the rules; they have to care about them. That only happens when they see leaders modeling those same standards under pressure.

I remember during one site visit, an auditor said to me, "Your policies are strong, but your people are stronger — they actually believe what they're doing matters." That was one of the best compliments an operations leader could receive.

Faith reminds me that compliance is really stewardship — the act of protecting what's been entrusted to your care. When leaders see it that way, the paperwork becomes purpose, not punishment.

Building Dynamic Compliance Programs

Now, let's be real. Regulations change faster than Kansas weather. (If this were an audiobook, you'd hear the nervous laughter of every compliance officer in America right about now.)

To stay ahead, compliance programs can't be static; they have to be living systems — flexible enough to adapt but structured enough to guide.

When I was in operational leadership, I implemented what I called "The Three P's": **Prepare, Prevent, and Pray.**

- **Prepare:** Stay informed. Regulations will change — that's a promise. Schedule regular check-ins to review HRSA, NCQA, and other governing updates.
- **Prevent:** Train often and document everything. Not because you don't trust your staff, but because clarity is the best insurance policy.
- **Pray:** Because sometimes, even after you've done all you can, an audit will still land on your desk at 4:59 p.m. on a Friday. (Ask me how I know.)

A compliance culture rooted in faith doesn't panic — it prepares. It stays teachable, humble, and proactive.

Strategic Risk Assessment and Mitigation

Risk is part of leadership; it's the price of growth. But unmanaged risk is a silent thief — it steals resources, credibility, and peace of mind.

Over the years, I've walked through enough crises to know that risk management isn't just about predicting what can go wrong —

it's about preparing your people for how to respond when it does.

In one organization I advised, a cyberattack nearly paralyzed their systems. The panic was real, but because we'd built a "crisis rhythm" — clear communication, assigned roles, and daily debriefs — they stabilized within days. Faith held the leaders steady while structure held the organization secure.

Faith doesn't erase risk; it reframes it. It asks, "What is this teaching us about our vulnerabilities, and how can we grow wiser from it?"

I often tell clients: **If you're praying for growth, pray for wisdom to handle what comes with it.** Every blessing carries responsibility, and every opportunity comes with risk. The goal isn't to avoid risk — it's to manage it faithfully.

Case Studies and Practical Insights
When Compliance Became Culture

I once worked with a community health organization that had fallen behind on regulatory reporting. Their leaders were talented and dedicated — they were just tired. Compliance felt like one more heavy task on an already overflowing plate. You could feel it in the air: the sigh before every meeting, the quiet dread when the word *audit* appeared in an email subject line. They weren't careless; they were human.

Instead of lecturing, I invited the leadership to see compliance through a new lens: *What if this isn't just about passing audits — what if it's about protecting people?*
That question landed differently. Suddenly, compliance wasn't a bureaucratic checklist — it was an act of care.

We began by listening. Each department listed the parts of compliance they dreaded most. One nurse said, "It feels like no matter what I do, it's never enough." Another manager admitted, "I know the rules, but I don't know *why* they matter in my day-to-day work." Those statements became our starting point.

We reframed compliance as a **shared value** rather than an obligation. Together, we developed a few simple practices that transformed how the team saw their work:

1. **Compliance Conversations:** Five-minute updates at every staff meeting where anyone could ask questions, share lessons, or celebrate small wins. ("We actually submitted on time this week — praise report!")

2. **Visible Victories Board:** A whiteboard in the break room listing completed reports, zero-finding audits, and shout-outs for staff who caught potential issues early. Seeing progress daily turned dread into momentum.

3. **The "Why Wall":** Posters reminding everyone *who* compliance protects — photos of patients, community events, and notes of thanks from families who benefited from the clinic's programs. Suddenly, policies had faces.

Within months, staff began catching and correcting issues themselves before leadership ever had to step in. Department heads started competing — in a healthy way — for who could close findings fastest.

Months later, when I followed up with this client, I was informed that when an auditor visited later that year, one of the front-desk staff proudly walked them through the new process like it was a tour of her home.

That's when I knew we'd crossed the line from compliance as *policy* to compliance as *culture*.

The atmosphere shifted. Laughter returned to meetings, I'm told. People started saying things like, "Let's do it right the first time — that's our standard now." The same team that once groaned at compliance emails was now drafting reminders for others.

And here's the deeper truth I carry from that experience:
When people understand that compliance protects lives, not paperwork, excellence becomes instinctive. You don't have to push people toward accountability — they start running toward it.

Faith played a quiet role too. During one meeting, a staff member said, "I guess this is really about stewardship, isn't it?" Exactly. Compliance is stewardship — of resources, of people, of trust. Once they made that connection, ownership took root.

There were still mistakes, of course (I like to think Yah allows them to keep us humble – if not, I'm in deep trouble). But mistakes became teachable moments instead of shameful ones. And that's when you know culture has changed: when correction feels like collaboration, not condemnation.

Faith in the Midst of Fire

There was another moment — one I'll never forget — when I wasn't the one inside the storm, but I could feel the heat from where I stood.

A client I'd worked with for over a year called me, voice trembling. Their organization had discovered a serious operational gap that threatened both their funding and their credibility with the community they served. It wasn't that they didn't care — they did. They'd even developed a beautiful, thorough plan months before... but it had stayed on the shelf, gathering dust under the weight of "more urgent" tasks.

Now, everything was urgent.
They weren't sure if they'd be able to continue serving their clients in the months ahead. The anxiety in that room was almost tangible — you could feel the mix of fear, regret, and exhaustion.

As a consultant, I've learned that sometimes my role is not to give orders, but to bring calm. So I took a deep breath and said, "Okay, let's start with what's true. You still have the plan. It's time to take it off the shelf and make it live."

We gathered the leadership team, pulled out that forgotten plan, and walked through it line by line. It wasn't perfect anymore — some parts needed updating, others needed courage to implement — but it was a start. Together, we turned panic into action:

- We established a timeline for immediate corrective steps.
- We divided responsibilities and set up accountability check-ins.
- We crafted a communication strategy that was honest, transparent, and compassionate.

The first meeting was hard. There were tears, awkward silences, and a few uncomfortable truths that had to be spoken out loud. But through it all, faith anchored the process.

At one point, I reminded them gently, "You were never being punished — you were being positioned. Sometimes, Yah allows the fire not to destroy what's weak, but to reveal what's strong."

They steadied themselves, owned their part, and began rebuilding — piece by piece, policy by policy, conversation by conversation.

When the follow-up review came, they didn't just pass — they excelled. The reviewers later shared that their corrective plan was being used as a model for others.

But that wasn't the real victory. The real victory was watching their confidence return — seeing leaders who had once been paralyzed by fear now walk in boldness and humility.

Faith didn't remove the fire; it refined them through it. And as their consultant, I didn't have to carry their flame — I just helped them remember where the light switch was.

Adapting Strategies Across Healthcare and Beyond

Compliance isn't a healthcare thing; it's a leadership thing. Whether you're running a clinic, a nonprofit, or a corporate division, the principle is the same: do the right thing *even when no one's watching.*

In consulting, I often find that organizations know the rules — what they lack is rhythm. They follow protocols but don't breathe purpose into them. So we start there. I ask leaders, "What does ethical excellence look like here?" And then we build systems around that answer.

I also remind them: **compliance without compassion becomes control** (I found out the hard way that this looks different to everyone). Rules are necessary, but relationships make them meaningful. The best policies are written by people who remember the faces behind the forms.

And on the lighter side — when your compliance officer smiles at a meeting, you know you're doing something right.

Conclusion

Navigating compliance and risk may never make the highlight reel of leadership, but it's where trust is built, integrity is proven, and faith gets tested.

When you approach it through a faith-driven lens, compliance becomes less about fear of failure and more about a commitment to faithfulness. Risk stops being a threat and becomes an opportunity to strengthen your foundation.

Here's what I know to be true:

- You can't control every outcome, but you can control your response (you can say that twice on Friday).
- You can't prevent every crisis, but you can prepare for it.
- You can't eliminate risk, but you can lead through it with courage, humility, and grace.

Faith-based compliance invites leaders to steward responsibility with conviction — to see every audit, every regulation, and every unexpected challenge as a chance to show excellence in motion.

So before you move on to the next chapter, pause for a moment and ask yourself:

When the unexpected happens, will fear drive your decisions, or will faith guide your response?

The way you answer that question will reveal not just your risk strategy — but your leadership legacy.

CHAPTER 6: FOSTERING INNOVATION AND QUALITY

Introduction

Innovation and quality are two words that get tossed around so often they can start to lose their meaning. But for me, they aren't buzzwords — they're promises.

When you've spent years leading in healthcare, you realize quickly that innovation isn't optional. It's survival. And quality? It's trust. Without it, everything else is just noise.

During my years leading an FQHC, I learned that innovation and quality don't grow in a vacuum. They grow in culture — one that welcomes new ideas, forgives honest mistakes, and celebrates learning. If people are afraid to speak up, you'll never hear the idea that could change everything.

Innovation and quality are sisters — one pushes boundaries, the other holds them steady. Together, they create excellence that lasts.

This chapter will explore what it takes to nurture both, through stories, lessons, and examples — not just from my leadership journey, but from the perspective of a woman who has prayed through more "innovative experiments" than I can count. (Some turned out wonderfully. Some... well, let's just say we learned a lot.)

Faith, humility, and curiosity — that's the real formula for innovation.

Cultivating Innovation

Creating an Environment Where Ideas Can Breathe

Innovation doesn't start with technology or funding — it starts with permission. The permission to ask "why," to question "how," and sometimes, to say "what if we tried something completely different?"

As a leader, I had to learn that not every new idea will be revolutionary — but every voice that's **brave** enough to speak up *could be.*

During my tenure as CEO at a Federally Qualified Health Center, I discovered that fostering innovation was less about adding new programs and more about removing fear. We created space — literally and figuratively — for creativity to live.

We created "round tables" where staff could share improvement suggestions without hierarchy in the room. Some ideas were practical ("can we make forms easier?"), others were visionary ("what if we had a mobile medical van?"). Many of those ideas became the backbone of new services.

Faith taught me that innovation is spiritual stewardship. You're not just managing what exists; you're birthing what could be.

Building an Innovative Culture

I'll never forget the COVID-19 pandemic. It was a masterclass in innovation and endurance.

When staffing shortages threatened our ability to provide care, we had to think differently. Traditional systems were breaking under pressure — and I could either panic or pray. (Spoiler alert: I did both – many saw the prayer, my mentor saw the temporary internal panic.)

That's when we reached out to the community. We partnered with off-duty Wichita firefighters to operate our mobile clinic and collaborated with the Wichita Black Nurses Association for medical outreach. Those partnerships didn't just fill staffing gaps — they redefined what community healthcare could look like.

We turned crisis into creativity. And it worked.

Faith played a major role in those decisions. Innovation wasn't about being flashy — it was about being faithful. We trusted that if we used what we had, Yah would multiply it.

Today, I bring that same mindset to my consultancy clients. When an organization tells me, "We can't afford to innovate," I gently remind them, "You can't afford *not* to." Innovation doesn't always require money — sometimes it just requires imagination and courage.

Practical Tips for Leaders Who Want to Spark Innovation

1. **Create Psychological Safety:** People won't share ideas if they're afraid of ridicule. Celebrate attempts, not just outcomes.
2. **Reward Curiosity:** Give recognition not only for success but for experimentation. ("We tried, it didn't work, but we learned something valuable.")

3. **Model Vulnerability:** Admit when you don't know (especially if you are the darn leader. It opens the door for someone else to teach you something new.

4. **Pray Before You Pivot:** Faith-based innovation invites discernment. Not every shiny idea is a divine one. Ask for wisdom before you act.

Leveraging Technology for Innovation
Technology as a Tool, Not a Trophy

I've seen organizations invest thousands — sometimes hundreds of thousands — in new systems that no one actually uses. The result? Fancy dashboards collecting digital dust.

Technology is not innovation by itself. It's a magnifier. It will amplify whatever already exists in your culture — excellence or confusion, collaboration or chaos. If your processes are messy, your tech will just make them messier faster.

When I led an FQHC, we struggled with patient flow and long wait times. The culprit? Disjointed data. We enhanced our electronic health record (EHR) system and reengineered the intake process. The outcome? Shorter wait times, fewer errors, and happier patients.

But here's what I loved most: the look of pride on the staff's faces when they saw the improvement data. They didn't just use the system — they *owned* it. Innovation had become personal.

Now, as a consultant, I help organizations do the same — aligning technology with mission, not the other way around. Before any implementation, I ask a few grounding questions:

- "What problem are we truly solving, and who benefits most?"

- "What is the human cost of this innovation?"
- "Have we prepared the people who will be most affected by it?"

Because technology without communication isn't progress — it's disruption disguised as development.

Recently, I observed a situation that reminded me just how high the stakes are when that communication doesn't happen. A leadership team became captivated by the promise of a new system — its automation, analytics, and all the efficiencies it could deliver. And to be fair, it was an impressive piece of technology. If implemented thoughtfully, it could absolutely strengthen the organization's operations.

But innovation isn't just about *what* a system can do; it's about *what it will cost* to make it work — and not only in dollars. The timelines were tight, the rollout was ambitious, and the human implications were left largely unspoken.

I'm not sure whether or not they implemented the system, but if they did, it probably delivered everything it promised — greater accuracy, faster output, improved reporting. But the emotional ripple effect would be just as real.

Some employees might quietly assume that the system is meant to replace those who aren't performing well.
And maybe, in some cases, that's partially true — every organization has areas where performance gaps exist. But when that message isn't clearly and compassionately communicated, fear doesn't just reach those who are underperforming — it spreads to those who *aren't*.

People who are excellent at their jobs start to worry that excellence won't matter anymore.

They begin protecting the parts of the work they love, uncertain if leadership still values them.

And the loyalty that once kept a team united begins to fracture into silence, whispers, and "wait and see."

That's the unintended cost of progress without communication.

The staff watching this unfold may not fully understand who leadership feels is ineffective or why. All they see is the quiet shift — a new system on the horizon and colleagues looking anxious. That uncertainty can create tension in the very teams you need most to champion the change.

The truth is, not everyone fears technology because they resist change; some fear it because they weren't invited to understand it.

When innovation is rolled out in secrecy or haste, it can make even your best employees second-guess their stability. They may start asking, "Am I next?" when the real question leadership meant to ask was, "How can we make this better?"

That's why communication is not just a courtesy — it's a safeguard. Transparency keeps fear from filling in the blanks.

I often tell leaders: **If your silence leaves space for imagination, imagination will usually build a monster.**

Faith reminds me that stewardship in leadership means preparing people, not surprising them. If the goal is accountability, lead with clarity. If the goal is excellence, explain the "why." And if the goal is transformation, honor the people who've carried you this far before asking them to carry something new.

If this system eventually went live, my hope is that it did so with wisdom — with clear expectations, transparent timelines, and meaningful engagement from the people it will most affect. Because when innovation walks hand in hand with empathy, even hard changes can become healing ones.

Technology should never be a threat to your people — it should be a testimony of your leadership.

And that's where faith steadies me most: it reminds me that excellence without empathy will always break something you meant to build. So before launching any new system, I still pause and pray —

"Father, help us to see beyond the promise of progress and remember the people who make it possible."

Because the measure of successful innovation isn't just how well the system works.
It's how well your people still feel seen when it does.

Faith, Technology, and the Human Touch
Faith keeps technology human.

It's easy to forget that every system, every dashboard, every report — behind it all are people. Real people. People whose names, stories, and data aren't just entries in a record; they're living testimonies.

I remind clients often that even the most advanced systems

can't replace compassion. Efficiency means nothing if empathy is lost along the way. You can automate reminders, but you can't automate kindness. You can build a dashboard for performance, but you can't quantify purpose.

One leader once joked, "V (only my friends call me that), you talk about these systems like it's a ministry." I laughed and said, "In a way, it is. It's how we steward information about people's lives." That usually earns a pause — and then a smile — because they realize I mean it. Every click, every report, every upload is a reflection of how seriously we take the privilege of caring for someone's most personal details.

When I was leading an FQHC, I used to tell my team, "If you touch a record, you've touched a life." That was our standard. Faith reframed data entry as discipleship — an act of integrity and excellence.

Faith reframes technology from a burden to a blessing — a tool to serve, not to dominate.
When we approach it that way, technology enhances care without erasing the heart behind it.

But here's where it gets tricky — sometimes we fall so in love with the promise of progress that we forget to ask whether the pace is still humane. We talk about *user experience* for patients but rarely about *user peace* for staff. If the technology improves outcomes but exhausts your people, is that still success?

Faith offers a kind of holy restraint in these moments — the courage to slow down and ask, "Is this system serving people or are people now serving the system?"

Because it's possible to be efficient and disconnected at the same time. It's possible to build technology so advanced that you lose sight of the faces it was meant to help.

In consulting, I see this tension often. Leaders want excellence (and rightly so), but sometimes they confuse excellence with speed. I remind them: excellence isn't how fast you implement a system; it's how faithfully you sustain it.

Faith calls us to see technology as an extension of ministry — a way to love people better, not a way to manage them faster.

And if you've ever worked in healthcare, you know what I mean — the moments that matter most are rarely in the data. They're in the pauses between the numbers. The nurse who takes an extra five minutes to comfort a patient. The case manager who remembers a client's child's name. The administrator who quietly prays over the day before the doors open.

Technology can track the visit, but it can't record the compassion. That's why faith remains essential — it keeps the work personal.

So yes, maybe I do sound like I'm talking about ministry when I talk about systems. Because for me, innovation is sacred when it serves humanity well.

Faith keeps us from idolizing technology. It teaches us to celebrate progress while still protecting peace, to value innovation without abandoning intimacy.

Because the future we're building isn't just digital — it's deeply human. And if faith has anything to say about it, it will stay that way.

Enhancing Quality

Quality as a Spiritual Commitment

Quality is more than metrics — it's a moral promise. When someone entrusts you with their care, their business, or their well-being, quality is how you honor that trust.

I've always believed that the pursuit of quality reveals what a leader truly values. It shows up in how we treat our people, how we communicate under pressure, and how we show up when no one's grading us. Quality is not the audit you pass — it's the integrity you practice between audits.

In my leadership years, I often said, *"Excellence is worship."* It raised a few eyebrows in early meetings (and once or twice, a polite cough from someone trying to process that line in a corporate setting). But I stood by it — because I meant it. To me, excellence is a form of gratitude. When we serve with care, precision, and compassion, we're saying "thank You" to the One who trusted us with the assignment in the first place.

You might also hear me say, *"The mercy you give is the mercy you receive."* That principle applies to leadership more than we realize. When we extend grace to our teams, our clients, our patients, and even ourselves during difficult seasons, that same grace has a way of finding its way back to us.

That mindset shaped how I approached our FQHC's journey toward accreditation. It wasn't just about passing inspections or earning another plaque for the lobby. It was about becoming *worthy* of the community's confidence. The process was grueling — policies, audits, documentation, sleepless nights — but each step refined us.

There were moments when I questioned whether we'd make it. (If this were an audiobook, you'd hear me laugh right here, because some of those nights were powered by prayer, coffee, and pure determination.) But as we pushed through, something shifted. The more we aligned our standards with our mission, the more our staff began to see quality not as "extra work," but as a shared expression of purpose.

When we finally achieved accreditation, it wasn't just a certificate on the wall — it was a declaration of faith and perseverance. Every department had contributed something sacred — their diligence, their patience, their prayers. The certificate symbolized something greater: that we had honored the trust of our patients and each other.

And that's what I teach now as a consultant — that quality isn't red tape; it's *refinement.* It's Yah's way of smoothing out the rough edges in both systems and souls.

I once worked with a client who dreaded their upcoming audit season. The word *audit* alone was enough to deflate morale. I could sense the anxiety building in the team. So I gathered them and said, "Let's change the language. We're not preparing for an audit; we're preparing to show what excellence looks like in motion."

That simple shift changed everything. They started approaching their work with pride instead of panic. Instead of asking, "What if we fail?" they began asking, "What can we improve?"

By the time the auditors arrived, the staff wasn't afraid — they were ready. Not because everything was perfect, but because they believed in what they were presenting.

Faith reframes quality from punishment to purpose. It reminds us that accountability is not something to fear — it's something to welcome. Because when we are accountable for the work, we become accountable to the calling.

Sometimes, quality is spiritual discipline disguised as documentation. It asks for patience, attention to detail, humility, and endurance. It requires us to keep showing up with integrity even when no one's clapping.

And when done right, it transforms not just the systems — but the spirit of the people within them.

Now, as a consultant, I help organizations see quality as something more than compliance. Quality is a culture. It's a way of saying, *"We care enough to do this right, even when no one's watching."*

Faith keeps that standard alive. Because when your quality reflects your Creator, your excellence will speak for itself.

Continuous Quality Improvement: The Power of Iteration

If you ever want to test a leader's patience, tell them "quality improvement is continuous."

Continuous means never done — and for results-oriented people, that can be frustrating.

But true quality lives in that tension between satisfaction and striving. Every process can be better; every service can be refined.

In one clinic I led, we used patient feedback and real-time analytics to track wait times. The numbers weren't flattering at first. (I think the staff called it "The Dashboard of Doom.") But over time, as we addressed bottlenecks and celebrated small wins, the culture shifted from shame to pride. The same dashboard that once caused groans became a motivator.

Faith reminded me: every critique is a chance to grow. Every data point is an invitation to improve.

Case Studies and Outcomes

Innovation at an FQHC

One of the proudest moments of my career came when our team achieved **National Committee for Quality Assurance (NCQA) recognition across every site we served** as a Federally Qualified Health Center. It was more than a milestone — it was a movement.

Reaching that level of accreditation required vision, discipline, and an extraordinary amount of heart. We didn't just earn the recognition; we *lived* it. The process touched every part of our operations — clinical workflows, data reporting, patient follow-up, care coordination — all of it had to be examined, refined, and rebuilt for sustainability.

It wasn't easy. There were moments when it felt like the goal kept moving faster than the finish line. But we stayed the course. The staff poured themselves into the work — nurses, providers, medical assistants, front desk teams, and administrators all rowing in the same direction.

And the best part? We didn't just achieve NCQA status once — we *maintained it.* Year after year, even on the day I walked away, those standards were still alive and thriving. That's the part that fills me with gratitude. Because true leadership isn't about what happens while you're there; it's about what still stands when you're gone.

That season taught me something profound about innovation: it's not just about creating something new; it's about sustaining something good.

We learned to marry innovation with accountability — to let creativity and compliance walk hand in hand. We built dashboards that didn't just track metrics but told the story of impact. We used data not as a whip, but as a window — a way to see where care could be better, faster, more compassionate.

The ripple effects were undeniable:

- Patient outcomes improved.
- Staff confidence grew.
- Community trust deepened.

That recognition wasn't simply a plaque on a wall — it was proof that faith, focus, and teamwork can elevate an entire organization.

Now, as a consultant, I carry that lesson into every engagement. When I help clients design their own systems of excellence, I remind them:

"You're not chasing awards — you're cultivating legacy."

Because at its core, innovation rooted in faith isn't about flash. It's about *fruit.* It's about building processes that honor people, systems that protect integrity, and standards that outlast leadership transitions.

I still tell my clients what I told my team back then:

"You're not just implementing structure — you're building stewardship."

That's the kind of innovation that multiplies impact far beyond the walls where it began — the kind that honors both purpose and people, leaving behind a standard that even time respects.

Quality Breakthrough in Healthcare Services

One of the most transformational experiences of my leadership journey was the development of our **Quality Assurance and Quality Improvement (QA/QI) Committee** — a cornerstone of every Federally Qualified Health Center, but one that we chose to treat as more than a requirement.

By HRSA standards, every FQHC must have a formal QA/QI program to evaluate, measure, and improve patient care and operational performance. But we wanted ours to be different — not just a compliance activity, but a *culture of accountability and ownership.*

So we built a committee that reflected the heart of the organization. We didn't limit participation to executives or clinicians; we opened the table to voices from every department — medical, dental, behavioral health, finance, outreach, and administration. We even had a board member and a patient representative — sometimes, beautifully, those roles were filled by the same person.

That mix changed everything.
When patients and staff sat side by side to discuss care processes, communication breakdowns, and opportunities for improvement, the conversations became real. We weren't talking about numbers; we were talking about *people.*

Each month, the committee met to review data, identify trends, and recommend solutions. But it didn't stop there — they also celebrated wins. A department that reduced no-show rates, a nurse who created a smoother triage process, a front desk clerk who spotted a recurring scheduling glitch — all of it mattered.

The results spoke for themselves:

- **Errors dropped** as processes became clearer and communication improved.
- **Morale rose** because people saw that their ideas actually led to change.
- **Silos dissolved** as departments began to understand how their work impacted others.
- **Engagement increased** because everyone — from the facilities team to the chief medical officer — saw themselves as part of the quality story.

Faith had a place in that room, too. Before difficult discussions, I'd often remind the committee, *"To handle this work with the care it deserves."* That reminder reframed the tone — it wasn't about blame; it was about stewardship.

The most meaningful moments weren't when an auditor complimented our reports — they were when a patient representative would say, "I can feel the difference in my care." That's when I knew the system was working exactly as it should — data and compassion, side by side.

Our QA/QI Committee became more than a governance requirement. It became a *movement* — a rhythm of reflection and refinement that connected every department to a shared purpose: to serve people with excellence.

And here's what I've learned since: quality doesn't improve because you create a policy — it improves because you create participation. When people are invited to be part of the solution, they'll protect it. When they understand the *why*, they'll sustain the *how*.

That's what makes quality contagious — not a program, but a posture.

Today, as a consultant, I help organizations build QA/QI programs with that same spirit. Yes, compliance matters — but culture is what keeps the standards alive long after the meeting ends. Because true quality doesn't start with paperwork — it starts with people who care enough to make it better, together.

And if you don't have a quality committee or team in place — and you're wondering why everyone in your organization isn't on the same page — you can start here. Create a space where people from every department can come together, share perspectives, and take ownership of improvement. You don't need a perfect plan to begin; you just need willing people and an open table. Start small, stay consistent, and watch how quickly alignment follows.

When quality becomes everyone's responsibility, excellence stops being something you chase — it becomes who you are.

Beyond Healthcare: Universal Lessons in Innovation and Quality

The principles of innovation and quality aren't bound to healthcare. They translate to every industry — from manufacturing to ministry, from classrooms to construction sites. Wherever people are trying to do something better, serve someone well, or build something that lasts, the lessons are the same.

Faith-based leadership brings a unique twist: we innovate with accountability. We take bold steps but stay tethered to purpose. We don't just ask, *"Can we do this?"* We ask, *"Should we — and if so, how do we do it with integrity?"*

Because innovation without integrity creates instability, and quality without compassion creates burnout.

I've watched business owners, educators, and nonprofit leaders all wrestle with the same balance — how to lead with vision without losing their values. The truth is, you can't separate the two. You can't sustain innovation without trust, and you can't build quality without care.

Whether you're building homes, running a restaurant, managing a church, or leading a Fortune 500 company, the secret is balance — faith in motion, strategy in action.

The details may differ, but the heart of the work is universal:

- **In construction**, quality means the home stands long after the builder walks away.
- **In education**, innovation means every student sees themselves as capable of learning.
- **In business**, integrity means the profit never outweighs the people.
- **In ministry**, excellence means representing Yahusha with consistency and love.

The industries change — but the assignment doesn't.

Faith-driven innovation asks us to build systems that serve humanity, not just productivity. It teaches leaders to pause long enough to ask, *"Who benefits from this decision, and who bears the weight of it?"*

Because whether you're managing patient charts or pouring concrete, excellence is still stewardship. So, if you've ever wondered how these principles apply to your world — start right where you are. Look at the systems around you, the people you lead, and the values you claim to hold. Ask yourself:

"Where can I innovate with integrity? Where can I raise the standard of quality without losing compassion?"

When faith leads the way, innovation becomes safer, and quality becomes sustainable.

And maybe that's the true universal lesson — that excellence isn't confined to any one field. It's the language of purpose wherever purpose lives.

Conclusion

Fostering innovation and quality requires courage, humility, and patience. It's not about perfection — it's about persistence.

Innovation keeps you fresh; quality keeps you faithful. Together, they ensure your organization serves not just efficiently, but excellently.

As a consultant and a woman of faith, I've seen what happens when leaders choose both: communities thrive, teams flourish, and impact deepens. So before you close this chapter, take a breath and ask yourself:

- Where have I stopped listening for new ideas?
- What process could I improve if I led with curiosity instead of criticism?
- And am I building systems that impress people — or systems that serve them?

Remember: excellence is never an accident. It's the daily decision to bring faith into function, vision into structure, and purpose into practice.

Innovation will push you. Quality will polish you.
But faith — faith will sustain you.

CONCLUSION

Summing Up the Journey: Leading with Purpose

If you've made it this far, first let me say — thank you. Truly.

You've walked with me through the valleys and mountaintops of leadership, faith, and the quiet, unglamorous moments in between. You've read the hard lessons, the unexpected breakthroughs, and probably caught a laugh or two along the way. (If you didn't laugh, please go back to Chapter 2 — I worked hard for those.)

"Leading with Purpose" was never meant to be a textbook — it's a *testimony*. It's the story of what happens when faith meets function, when heart meets strategy, and when leadership becomes less about hierarchy and more about stewardship.

Each chapter has been a thread, and together they've woven a tapestry — one that reflects not perfection, but purpose in motion.

A Tapestry of Leadership Lessons

1. Faith-Driven Leadership:

We began where all true leadership begins — at the intersection of faith and responsibility. Faith doesn't make leadership easier; it makes it meaningful. It gives leaders the courage to do what's right when it's inconvenient, to love people when it's hard, and to see purpose where others see pressure. We learned that faith isn't just a moral compass — it's a stabilizing force, shaping organizations into communities that operate with integrity and heart.

2. Strategic Planning and Execution:

Then we moved from the heart to the head — the work of planning, executing, and adjusting. We explored how strategy, when led by conviction, becomes more than a roadmap — it becomes a mirror of leadership's character. We talked about aligning mission with methods, people with purpose, and courage with consistency. Because plans may change, but principles never should.

3. Empathy and Executive Coaching:

Here we slowed down and looked inward. We talked about empathy not as a soft skill but as a superpower. Coaching with empathy builds leaders who don't just perform — they *transform.* We discovered that empathy is the bridge between authority and authenticity, allowing leaders to connect deeply while still holding accountability high. (And yes, it's also the secret ingredient to surviving team meetings on a Monday morning.)

4. Operational Excellence:

Next, we put our hands to the work — where leadership meets logistics. We uncovered that operational excellence is not about perfection; it's about *presence.* It's showing up consistently, doing the small things well, and protecting the culture that keeps systems strong. We learned that excellence doesn't mean doing everything — it means doing the right things with faith and focus.

5. Navigating Compliance and Risk:

From there, we stepped into the world of policies, regulations, and all the things that can keep leaders up at night. (If you've ever survived an audit, you know what I mean.) We reframed compliance from fear to faithfulness — understanding it as stewardship, not restriction. And we learned that risk management, when guided by integrity and communication, doesn't suffocate innovation — it sustains it.

6. Fostering Innovation and Quality:

Finally, we explored the beautiful tension between creativity and consistency — how innovation and quality can coexist when rooted in faith. We saw that innovation isn't about chasing trends;

it's about solving real problems with wisdom and compassion. And quality, when viewed as a spiritual commitment, becomes worship in motion — the daily act of honoring the people who trust us with their lives, their resources, and their hopes.

Forward, Together

If you take nothing else from these pages, take this: leadership isn't about titles, followers, or fancy systems. It's about *trust.* It's about showing up when it's hard, being honest when it's costly, and believing that faith and excellence are not opposites — they're partners.

"Leading with Purpose" is not a manual — it's an invitation. A call to lead boldly, to think differently, and to remember that your work — whatever your industry — is holy ground when done with integrity.

The lessons shared here were born from both success and failure — the kind that stretches your patience, tests your calling, and refines your purpose. But if there's one thing I know, it's this: nothing in your journey will be wasted if you let faith guide the process.

I wrote this book not as someone who's figured it all out, but as someone who's been through enough to know what matters. And what matters most is people — the ones you serve, the ones you lead, and the ones who quietly carry the mission when no one's watching.

So as you close this book, pause for a moment and ask yourself:

- What will leadership look like for me now?
- What legacy am I quietly building in the choices I make today?
- And how can I make sure faith remains the thread that

holds it all together?

The truth is, this book is just the *beginning.* Leadership is a living journey — one that keeps unfolding, testing, and teaching us.

The ideas and strategies within these pages are here to spark your imagination and strengthen your foundation. But the next chapter — *your chapter* — is written through action.

If you're ready to keep growing, to stretch your capacity, and to lead with greater clarity and conviction, I would be honored to walk with you further. Through my consultancy, my team can help leaders and organizations turn purpose into performance — aligning strategy with soul, compliance with compassion, and excellence with endurance. Together, we can build the systems, culture, and impact that your mission deserves.

LEADING BEYOND THESE PAGES

As we close this chapter — and open new ones in your own story — remember:
True leadership is never about being in charge; it's about being entrusted.

Lead with humility, but don't hide your brilliance.
Innovate boldly, but stay anchored in faith.
Pursue excellence, but never forget grace.

Because the legacy of leadership isn't measured in titles or timelines — it's measured in *transformation.*

So go forward — wiser, braver, and more grounded than before.
Lead with purpose.
Live with conviction.
And let your faith be the force that lights the way.

Thank you for walking this path with me.
Now, let's lead — together.

EPILOGUE: A JOURNEY WITH VENUS LEE

Imagine yourself as a high-powered executive, facing a critical juncture in your career. Your organization is at a crossroads, and despite your best efforts, the challenges seem insurmountable. The stakes are high, and your leadership is being tested like never before. This is the perfect moment for a transformative experience, one that could reshape not only your professional trajectory but the future of your entire organization.

In this scenario, you find yourself staring at the boardroom ceiling after another late-night meeting. The usual confidence that carried you through countless business deals and strategic decisions now feels like a distant memory. Your team is demoralized, and the company's performance metrics are slipping. Something has to change, but what? That's when you remember a recommendation from a trusted colleague about a consultant who specializes in turning around tough situations with a blend of strategic acumen and empathetic leadership.

Enter Venus Lee, a name that resonates with authority and a reputation for transforming organizations. With a blend of faith-driven principles and a keen understanding of business dynamics, Venus offers something different—something more profound than just another business consultant.

You decide to reach out, and soon, you're on a call with Venus. Her voice is both calming and confident, exuding a sense of purpose and direction. She listens intently as you pour out your concerns and frustrations, her empathy palpable even over the phone. By the end of the call, you feel a spark of hope. This isn't just about fixing problems; it's about reigniting a passion for leadership and creating a culture of excellence.

The next week, Venus walks into your office, her presence commanding yet approachable. She's here to not only guide but to partner with you on this journey. Her insights are sharp, her strategies innovative, and her approach deeply rooted in ethical leadership. Together, you dissect the issues, unraveling layers of complexities with surgical precision. Venus's methods are not just practical; they're transformative, blending data-driven strategies with a profound understanding of human dynamics.

One by one, the barriers begin to crumble. The team meetings, once fraught with tension, start to buzz with renewed energy and optimism. Venus's emphasis on empathy and faith-driven leadership fosters a sense of unity and purpose among your staff. Her strategic planning sessions reveal new opportunities, previously obscured by the fog of crisis. Her operational insights streamline processes, bringing efficiency and clarity.

As the months pass, the results are undeniable. Your organization not only recovers but begins to thrive in ways you hadn't imagined. The boardroom, once a place of stress and conflict, now echoes with success stories and forward-looking strategies. Your team, once fragmented and disheartened, now operates as a cohesive unit, driven by shared goals and a renewed sense of purpose.

Throughout this journey, Venus remains a steadfast guide, her faith and wisdom illuminating the path. She doesn't just provide solutions; she empowers you to become the leader you were always meant to be. Her guidance is a blend of tough love and unwavering support, pushing you to achieve excellence while always having your back.

The transformation is complete, but the journey continues. As you sit in your office, reflecting on the remarkable turnaround, you realize that the true value of this experience isn't just in the improved metrics or the accolades. It's in the profound personal growth you've undergone, the lessons learned, and the unshakeable belief in your ability to lead with purpose and integrity.

You reach for the phone, ready to take the next step. This time, it's not about crisis management but about seizing new opportunities and continuing the journey of excellence. As you dial Venus's number, a sense of excitement and anticipation fills you. You're not just calling a consultant; you're reconnecting with a partner in your journey towards greatness.

"Venus," you say as she answers, "let's take this journey together."

And with that, a new chapter begins, filled with promise, purpose, and the unwavering belief that, with the right guidance, there are no limits to what you can achieve.

APPENDICES

Appendix A: Further Reading and Exploration To continue your journey in leadership and organizational development, explore the following resources, which will provide you with a broader understanding and additional insights:

1. **Purposeful Leadership Insights:** Visit our continually updated blog for articles, case studies, and the latest insights on leadership, operational excellence, and more. As we continue to grow, you will be able to engage with a community of thought leaders and practitioners dedicated to transforming the landscape of business leadership. **Purposeful Leadership Insights**

2. **Recommended Books and Articles:**
   - **Leaders Eat Last** by Simon Sinek: Explore the importance of creating a culture of trust and commitment within organizations.
   - **Good to Great** by Jim Collins: Learn about the principles that help companies transition from being good companies to great ones.
   - **The Five Dysfunctions of a Team** by Patrick Lencioni: Understand common hurdles that teams face and strategies to overcome them.

3. **Professional Journals:**
   - **Harvard Business Review:** Access a wide range of articles on leadership and management practices that are at the forefront of research and practical application.
   - **Journal of Business Ethics:** Explore various

aspects of ethics in business, providing a deep dive into the moral complexities of leadership and corporate governance.

Disclaimer: The materials listed above are provided for thought-provoking purposes and to evoke a diversity of ideas in the realm of business leadership. I do not necessarily endorse all the viewpoints or methodologies presented in the recommended readings, except for the content found on my personal blog, "Purposeful Leadership Insights." My aim is to encourage diverse perspectives and critical thinking as you continue to develop your leadership skills and strategies.

APPENDIX B — THE LEADERSHIP COVENANT:

A Letter to Those Who Lead with Faith

A LETTER FROM VENUS

To the leader reading this — the one still showing up, still believing, and still trying to do what's right even when no one's watching: **I see you.**
I've been you.

Leadership is beautiful, but it isn't always glamorous. There are days when it feels like purpose and pressure are having a tug-of-war in your chest. There are seasons when you'll wonder if your voice even matters.
But let me remind you — if you are still standing, still caring, still trying — **it matters.**

Faith-driven leadership was never meant to be perfect; it was meant to be *present.*
You won't always get it right. You'll make tough calls that others won't understand. You'll have to forgive when it feels unfair and lead when you'd rather retreat. But each time you choose integrity over impulse, compassion over convenience, and courage over comfort — Heaven takes note.

You are shaping more than outcomes — you're shaping culture, hope, and healing.

So breathe.

Refocus.
Remember why you started.

This work you do — whether in healthcare, business, education, or ministry — is holy ground when done with love and excellence.
You are not here by accident.
You are an answer to someone's prayer for a better leader.

When the load feels heavy, **rest before you quit.**
Pray before you panic.
And keep your faith at the center of your strategy.

You were made for *impact,* not *applause.*
And you are doing better than you think.

With love and belief,
Venus Lee
Founder, *Venus Lee & Associates*
www.VenusLeeandAssociates.com

THE LEADERSHIP COVENANT

This covenant is a reflection — a personal promise to yourself, your team, and the purpose you've been called to fulfill.

Read it slowly. Speak it aloud. Sign it if it resonates with you.

I will lead with faith before fear.
I will choose people over pride and purpose over pressure.
I will treat excellence as worship and humility as strength.
I will listen before I lead, and serve before I speak.
I will innovate with integrity, build with compassion, and correct with grace.
I will remember that leadership is not about power — it's about stewardship.

When the work feels heavy, I will pause, pray, and remember:

I was chosen for this assignment not because I am perfect, but because I am willing.

Signed:

_____

ABOUT THE AUTHOR

Venus Lee is a respected consultant, author, and leadership expert based in Wichita, Kansas, with more than three decades of experience transforming organizations across healthcare, nonprofit, and corporate sectors. As the Founder and Principal Consultant of Venus Lee & Associates, she has dedicated her life's work to helping leaders and teams operate with excellence — not just through systems and strategy, but through purpose and faith.

Her approach to leadership is grounded in a simple but powerful belief: *excellence is worship.* For Venus, leadership is not about titles or accolades — it's about stewardship, character, and impact. Through her consultancy, she guides organizations to align strategic innovation, operational efficiency, and ethical integrity with a deeper sense of calling.

Much of her work has centered around Federally Qualified Health Centers (FQHCs), where she has developed programs and systems that strengthened community care, enhanced operational effectiveness, and built sustainable models for growth. Her leadership has inspired measurable results — from improving patient outcomes and reducing costs to fostering cultures of compassion and accountability.

A Kansas native with a compelling story of resilience and grace, Venus has weathered public challenges that tested both her faith and her leadership philosophy. Those experiences refined her purpose. Rather than dimming her light, they deepened it.

Today, she uses her story to remind others that adversity doesn't define us — it develops us. Her journey stands as living proof that integrity and faith are powerful anchors, even in turbulent seasons.

Throughout her distinguished career, Venus has held multiple executive roles — including Chief Executive Officer, Chief Operations Officer, Chief Financial Officer, and Associate Executive Officer — leading major initiatives that changed the landscape of community health. Under her leadership at one FQHC, she oversaw the launch of three pharmacies, a pioneering medical-legal partnership, and multiple in-house programs that expanded access to holistic care. At another, her operational reforms helped eliminate debt, reduce inventory costs, and strengthen efficiency across the organization.

Her influence extends beyond healthcare. Venus has served on numerous boards, including the Quivira Council of the Boy Scouts of America, the UnitedHealthcare National FQHC Advisory Board, the Wichita Rotary Club, and the American College of Healthcare Executives (ACHE), among others.

Her work has been widely recognized, earning her several prestigious honors such as the Excellence in Health Care Administration Award (2020), the Diversity and Inclusion Award (2020), the Women Who've Changed the Heart of the City Award – Topeka (2020), the Women Who Lead: Major Companies Award (2021), and the Wichita Business Journal Executive of the Year Award (2021).

Beyond her executive and consulting achievements, Venus is a teacher at heart — a speaker and thought leader who has inspired audiences through workshops, seminars, and her blog, *Purposeful Leadership Insights.* Her writing bridges professional excellence with personal growth, faith, and purpose, making her a trusted voice for those who want to lead well and live well.

As an author, Venus brings her wisdom, wit, and faith together in *Leading with Purpose: Executive Insights for Business Success and Personal Growth*, distilling a lifetime of lessons into a guide for leaders seeking to integrate values, vision, and vitality. Her message is simple but enduring:

Leadership is not about climbing higher — it's about digging deeper.

Through every role, every challenge, and every victory, Venus Lee continues to champion a form of leadership that transcends industries and transforms lives — one decision, one team, and one purpose at a time.

www.ingramcontent.com/pod-product-compliance
Lightning Source LLC
Chambersburg PA
CBHW070116230526
45472CB00004B/1276